Copyright © 2025 by Pocketlings
ISBN: 978-1-0693332-3-0

All rights reserved. No part of this publication, either writing or images, may be reproduced, distributed, or transmitted in any form or by any means, including photocopying, recording, or other electronic or mechanical methods, without the prior written permission of the publisher, except in the case of brief quotations embodied in critical reviews and certain other noncommercial uses permitted by copyright law.
Published by Zenblank © 2025

Hey you!

Yup—you! Just wanted to say... you're awesome. Like, seriously awesome.
This book? It's just for kids like us—who dream big, feel big, and do big things (even if adults don't always get it).
So let's play, draw, laugh, think, and do all the fun stuff together.

No pressure. No tests. Just awesomeness.

Ready? Let's gooo!

– Olamide

Welcome

Hi friend!
We're the Pocketlings—plush dolls full of big joy, big dreams, and even bigger love.

In this book, you'll find fun games, awesome affirmations, and cool little challenges to help you remember just how amazing you are. It's not about being perfect—it's about being YOU.

So get cozy, grab a pencil (or crayons!), and let's go on an adventure filled with confidence, kindness, and a whole lot of fun.

We're so glad you're here.

—Your Pocketlings pals

"I am **AUDACIOUS**, brave enough to take bold risks and try new things that others might find too difficult."

Audacious is an adjective describing someone willing to take surprisingly bold risks; it comes from Latin 'audacia' meaning courage.

"I am ASTUTE, quick to notice important details that others might miss."

Astute is an adjective from Latin 'astutus' meaning crafty; it describes someone who shows sharp mental cleverness and good judgment.

Benevolent is an adjective from Latin 'bene' (good) and 'volent' (wishing); it describes someone who actively wishes good things for others.

"I am BENEVOLENT, choosing kindness and wanting to help others whenever I can."

"I am CAPTIVATING, able to charm and fascinate people with my unique ideas and personality."

Captivating is a present participle used as an adjective; it literally means "taking captive" but is used figuratively to describe someone who holds others' attention completely.

"I am **DISCERNING**, able to judge well and make thoughtful choices by seeing important differences that others might miss."

Discerning is an adjective from Latin 'discernere' meaning 'to separate' or 'to distinguish'; it describes someone with good judgment who can recognize subtle distinctions and make wise choices based on careful observation.

"I am EMPOWERED, filled with the strength and confidence to make my own choices and create positive change."

Empowered is a past participle used as an adjective; it describes someone who has been given the authority or ability to do something, from the root word 'power' combined with the prefix 'em-' meaning 'to put into'.

"I am FELICITOUS, naturally skilled at choosing just the right words and actions for each situation."

Felicitous is an adjective from Latin 'felix' meaning happy or fortunate; it describes someone or something that is well-suited or especially appropriate to the occasion.

Galvanizing is a present participle used as an adjective; it comes from the name of Italian scientist Luigi Galvani and literally refers to stimulating muscles through electricity, but figuratively means to shock or excite someone into taking action.

"I am GALVANIZING, able to excite and inspire others to take action with my energy and enthusiasm."

Complete the crossword puzzle below (A–I)

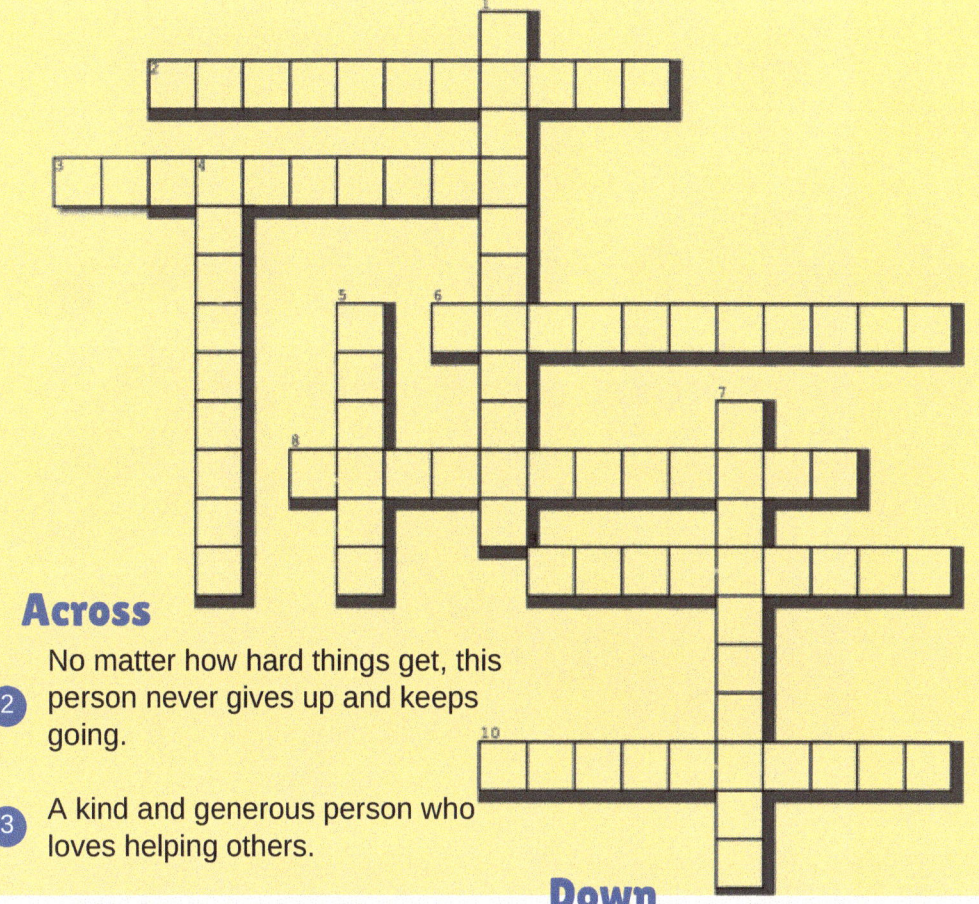

Across

2. No matter how hard things get, this person never gives up and keeps going.

3. A kind and generous person who loves helping others.

6. Something that makes people excited and ready to take action.

8. This person helps people in need, like giving food to the hungry or helping in a disaster.

9. This person is bold and not afraid to take risks, even if it seems scary.

10. Something that is perfect for the moment and makes people happy.

Down

1. Something so interesting and exciting that you can't stop looking or listening.

4. Feeling strong and confident to do something on your own.

5. Someone who is very clever and can figure things out quickly.

7. A person who can tell the difference between good and bad choices very easily.

Affirmation Adventure: The Power of Positive Words! 🌟💪

How to Play:

Instead of using negative or discouraging words, fill in the blanks with positive, empowering words from the list below! These words will remind you how awesome and strong you are!

Words to Use (Synonyms for Encouragement!):

1. Resilient (Instead of saying "I can't handle this," say "I am strong and can bounce back!")

2. Tenacious (Instead of saying "This is too hard," say "I never give up!")

3. Empowered (Instead of saying "I'm not good enough," say "I believe in myself!")

4. Wondrous (Instead of saying "Nothing ever excites me," say "Life is full of amazing things!")

5. Observant (Instead of saying "I don't understand," say "I notice things others miss!")

6. Captivating (Instead of saying "I'm boring," say "I have something special to share!")

The Adventure of the Lost Treasure! 🏆 🌍

Olayemi had always dreamed of becoming an explorer. One day, she discovered an ancient map leading to a hidden treasure! But before she could reach it, she had to face a series of challenges.

First, she had to solve a tricky puzzle. At first, Olayemi felt frustrated, but then she reminded herself, "I am (1) _____, and I always find a way to solve problems!"

Next, she had to cross a deep river. The waves were strong, but Olayemi took a deep breath and said, "I am (2) _____, and I never give up, no matter how tough things get!"

As she traveled further, she found a glowing cave filled with sparkling crystals. "This place is truly (3) _____," Olayemi whispered in awe.

Deep inside the cave, she found an ancient scroll with clues. Most people would have missed the tiny details, but Olayemi knew, "I am (4) _____, and I notice things that others don't."

Finally, after a long journey, Olayemi stood before the legendary treasure chest. It wasn't filled with gold—it was filled with books, art, and stories from the past! Olayemi smiled, knowing that she had found something even more (5) _____ than riches.

With confidence, Olayemi stepped forward and thought, "I am (6) _____, and my story is worth sharing with the world!"

🎉 **Your Challenge:** Fill in the blanks with the words from the list and read your completed story out loud. Let these words remind you how strong, smart, and amazing you are!

✨ **Bonus Challenge:** Draw your own treasure map and create an adventure where YOU are the hero!

Word Unscramble Challenge 1

Can you unscramble these words? Use the clues (word definitions) to help you solve them.

Scrambled Words & Clues

1. **nstrevOba** – Someone who notices small details that others might miss.

2. **Flocueisit** – Something that is perfect for the moment and makes people happy.

3. **oetenvelBn** – A kind and generous person who loves helping others.

4. **yiineahLrbnt** – Something tricky and complicated, like a giant maze.

5. **oapiNlner** – Someone or something that is the best with no equal.

6. **sicduuoJi** – Someone who makes smart choices and thinks before acting.

7. **mEoeepwrd** – Feeling strong and confident to do something big.

8. **uacVseiro** – A person who always tells the truth.

How to Play

- Unscramble each word to find the real word.
- Use the clues (word definitions) to help you.
- Once you solve them all, try using each word in your own sentence.

Bonus Challenge: Write a short story using at least three of the words from any set.

"I am HUMANITARIAN, showing compassion toward others and working to make the world better for everyone."

Humanitarian is both a noun and an adjective derived from 'human'; it describes someone who promotes human welfare and social reforms, emphasizing our shared humanity rather than differences.

Indomitable is an adjective from Latin 'in-' (not) and 'domitare' (to tame); it describes someone who cannot be subdued or overcome, suggesting inner strength that persists despite obstacles.

"I am INDOMITABLE, facing challenges with a spirit that cannot be defeated or discouraged."

"I am **JUDICIOUS**, thinking carefully before making decisions and considering what is fair and wise."

Judicious is an adjective related to the word 'judge'; it describes someone who shows good judgment or sense, carefully weighing options before acting rather than rushing to conclusions.

"I am KNOWLEDGEABLE, filled with useful information and understanding that I can share with others."

Knowledgeable is an adjective formed by adding the suffix '–able' to 'knowledge'; it describes someone who possesses a wide range of information or understanding about many subjects.

"I am LABYRINTHINE, complex and interesting with many twists and turns to my thoughts and ideas."

Labyrinthine is an adjective derived from 'labyrinth,' referring to the ancient Greek maze; it describes something intricate and complicated in structure, suggesting depth and fascinating complexity rather than confusion.

Multifaceted combines 'multi-' (many) with 'facet' (small surface); it describes someone with many dimensions or aspects to their character, suggesting richness and complexity that makes them interesting.

"I am MULTIFACETED, showing many different talents and sides to my personality like a beautifully cut gemstone."

Word Search 1

D	P	I	W	N	W	N	O	N	P	A	R	E	I	L	C	Z	G	W	R	W	V
N	E	W	C	H	O	O	N	P	P	C	F	P	W	V	S	I	C	R	J	I	G
Y	S	N	W	P	D	O	Z	N	D	E	R	E	W	O	P	M	E	A	N	T	N
J	F	U	I	T	I	J	X	J	G	K	A	S	T	U	T	E	C	D	M	I	I
Y	Q	O	O	H	U	K	O	Y	V	B	P	P	D	F	S	Y	O	U	X	U	T
J	V	H	B	I	T	C	R	Y	K	T	J	N	X	T	C	M	K	I	E	D	A
W	F	D	W	A	C	N	V	S	V	W	Z	F	L	D	I	D	V	D	X	J	V
G	A	E	G	K	X	I	I	A	Q	E	S	S	E	T	B	W	K	M	O	Z	I
A	G	T	S	R	N	F	D	R	N	A	I	R	A	T	I	N	A	M	U	H	T
U	A	E	C	R	E	G	S	U	Y	Y	Z	B	V	S	C	R	A	T	H	O	P
D	F	C	G	G	L	J	O	R	J	B	L	H	U	N	K	W	I	F	T	E	A
A	V	A	A	T	B	P	H	K	O	E	A	O	E	Q	P	V	Z	S	U	T	C
C	K	F	L	G	A	E	O	B	U	F	E	L	I	C	I	T	O	U	S	X	A
I	X	I	V	T	E	S	N	Q	I	B	K	X	T	A	J	N	O	M	N	B	W
O	X	T	A	I	G	I	D	E	C	D	G	I	Q	V	A	H	L	V	N	I	T
U	P	L	N	M	D	D	V	K	V	F	N	R	P	C	K	J	M	I	H	M
S	K	U	I	K	E	H	H	A	F	O	V	W	Z	H	K	A	C	M	A	M	I
D	D	M	Z	T	L	F	T	N	X	J	L	C	Y	C	Y	K	B	L	S	L	P
G	S	I	I	E	W	C	C	Q	Q	I	O	E	N	W	K	W	R	C	S	O	J
B	I	X	N	F	O	I	H	V	G	H	K	N	R	S	Q	X	U	O	U	O
J	K	L	G	W	N	P	X	W	Z	A	R	K	H	T	T	L	P	O	S	O	T
T	V	T	V	X	K	N	O	T	X	T	X	S	K	Q	S	E	N	W	V	J	D

AUDACIOUS	HUMANITARIAN
ASTUTE	INDOMITABLE
BENEVOLENT	JUDICIOUS
CAPTIVATING	KNOWLEDGEABLE
EMPOWERED	LABYRINTHINE
FELICITOUS	MULTIFACETED
GALVANIZING	NONPAREIL

How to Play:

1. **Find the Words:** Look for words hidden in the letter grid.

2. **Words Go Different Ways:** Words can go across, up and down, or diagonally. They can even be spelled backwards!

3. **Mark the Words:** When you find a word, circle it with a crayon or pencil.

4. **Tip:** Start by looking for the first letter of each word.

5. **You Win:** When you find all the words!

6. The words to look for are above

Affirmation Quest: The Magic of Positive Words! ✨💡

How to Play:
Instead of using negative words when things feel tough, fill in the blanks with positive, powerful words from the list below! These words will remind you how incredible you are!

Words to Use (Encouraging Synonyms!):

1. Audacious (Instead of saying "I'm afraid to try," say "I am bold and ready for adventure!")

2. Discerning (Instead of saying "I don't know what to do," say "I make smart choices!")

3. Galvanizing (Instead of saying "I feel unmotivated," say "I can inspire myself and others!")

4. Quintessential (Instead of saying "I don't matter," say "I am the perfect version of myself!")

5. Veracious (Instead of saying "I don't have anything important to say," say "My words are honest and powerful!")

6. Xenodochial (Instead of saying "I don't fit in," say "I am kind and welcoming to others!")

The Hero's Journey!

Once upon a time, in a kingdom of endless stars, a young hero named Olabisi set out on a great adventure. She wasn't sure if she was ready, but they reminded themselves, "I am (1) _____, and I am brave enough to take on any challenge!"

As Olabisi traveled through enchanted lands, they had to make an important choice—one that would shape their journey forever. She took a deep breath and said, "I am (2) _____, and I trust myself to make the best decision."

Suddenly, Olabisi reached a town where the people had lost her hope. She had forgotten how to dream big! But Olabisi stood tall and said, "I am (3) _____, and I can spark excitement and courage in others!"

The villagers cheered, and an old wise woman approached Olabisi. "You," she said, "are the (4) _____ hero we have been waiting for—the perfect example of bravery and kindness."

Olabisi smiled, knowing her words had meaning. "I am (5) _____," she thought. "I speak with truth and confidence because my voice matters."

With new friends by her side, Olabisi continued her adventure, knowing that she was (6) _____, always open-hearted and welcoming to those they met along the way.

And so, her story became legendary, passed down for generations.

🎉 **Your Challenge:** Fill in the blanks with the words from the list and read your completed story out loud. Let these words remind you of your own strength, courage, and kindness!

✨ **Bonus Challenge:** Create your own magical adventure using these words! Draw a picture of yourself as the hero!

Word Unscramble Challenge 2

Can you unscramble these words? Use the clues (word definitions) to help you solve them.

Scrambled Words & Clues

1. **aSintpe** – A person who is very wise and full of knowledge.

2. **ieouariPpcscs** – Someone who understands things quickly and clearly.

3. **stAtue** – Someone who is clever and can figure things out fast.

4. **oausucidA** – Someone who is bold and not afraid to take risks.
   oceiZt – Full of life and energy.

5. **Rtlisneie** – Someone who stays strong, even when things get tough.

6. **zlanvniGgai** – Something that excites and inspires people to take action.

7. **vitpaitnagC** – So interesting that people can't stop watching or listening.

How to Play

- Unscramble each word to find the real word.
- Use the clues (word definitions) to help you.
- Once you solve them all, try using each word in your own sentence.

Bonus Challenge: Write a short story using at least three of the words from any set.

Word Search 2

J	J	Y	M	Q	A	E	Z	Z	O	J	S	V	A	R	T	Z	P	Q	W	P	T
P	V	U	M	V	O	I	Q	X	M	S	U	O	I	C	A	N	E	T	Y	C	Q
N	Q	K	K	O	G	Z	J	N	W	C	W	Z	A	S	M	P	P	Z	P	U	Q
Y	S	M	O	M	F	R	Q	R	C	O	F	C	A	N	I	N	P	U	I	X	I
S	A	J	P	B	R	B	I	F	K	R	B	M	H	I	R	P	H	N	S	V	E
E	U	R	K	T	F	D	F	H	B	G	Z	S	A	D	E	D	T	N	H	H	D
U	F	O	E	J	M	Z	W	S	I	C	S	C	E	R	F	E	Z	R	V	E	J
C	V	R	R	B	S	Q	M	S	K	E	J	B	S	R	S	L	C	Z	U	X	H
P	D	J	E	D	Z	J	G	K	U	B	D	P	H	S	V	C	W	V	L	E	Q
Q	P	R	N	L	N	F	B	W	I	O	I	V	E	B	J	A	F	H	B	N	F
X	Z	N	Z	Z	B	O	Z	D	A	C	I	N	X	L	E	B	N	X	C	O	M
U	U	R	J	R	Z	A	W	Q	A	Q	T	C	J	A	X	M	H	T	M	D	H
P	X	E	V	G	Y	Q	M	C	E	I	R	R	A	T	B	U	U	L	C	O	Q
B	T	S	R	M	U	T	I	O	A	W	I	E	V	R	G	Y	Z	G	G	C	S
G	Y	I	U	Q	E	O	N	L	H	X	T	Y	I	X	E	I	W	T	A	H	V
E	D	L	M	T	U	Q	Z	E	V	T	Q	H	I	D	Z	V	B	T	I	I	N
X	R	I	T	S	Z	E	Q	U	I	Q	A	I	E	S	O	J	J	I	Q	A	M
A	Y	E	K	G	U	O	L	N	R	P	I	F	H	Y	H	W	W	D	G	L	L
M	S	N	O	Z	X	D	E	B	K	S	A	A	N	R	O	Q	Y	W	K	I	H
Z	S	T	E	U	V	U	U	T	L	Z	Y	S	N	U	D	W	V	N	I	M	S
U	E	W	U	A	G	H	A	L	I	D	Z	V	P	E	C	M	I	E	P	I	T
V	I	P	L	P	S	R	G	A	Z	C	H	V	Y	V	S	N	N	U	R	F	J

OBSERVANT	UNFATHOMABLE
PERSPICACIOUS	VERACIOUS
QUINTESSENTIAL	WONDROUS
RESILIENT	XENODOCHIAL
SAPIENT	YARE
TENACIOUS	ZOETIC
OBSERVANT	UNFATHOMABLE

How to Play:

7 **Find the Words:** Look for words hidden in the letter grid.

8 **Words Go Different Ways:** Words can go across, up and down, or diagonally. They can even be spelled backwards!

9 **Mark the Words:** When you find a word, circle it with a crayon or pencil.

10 **Tip:** Start by looking for the first letter of each word.

11 **You Win:** When you find all the words!

12 The words to look for are above

"I am NONPAREIL, unique and without equal in my special gifts and talents." Nonpareil is an adjective from French meaning 'having no equal'; it describes someone or something so exceptional that nothing else can be compared to it, emphasizing the value of individual uniqueness.

"I am OBSERVANT, noticing small details and changes that others might miss in the world around me."

Observant is an adjective from Latin 'observare' meaning 'to watch'; it describes someone who pays careful attention to details, suggesting both awareness and thoughtfulness about one's surroundings.

Perspicacious is an adjective from Latin 'perspicax' meaning 'sharp-sighted'; it describes someone with unusually astute perception or understanding, suggesting an ability to see beyond surface appearances to deeper truths.

"I am PERSPICACIOUS, seeing clearly through confusing situations with my keen insight and understanding."

"I am **QUINTESSENTIAL**, representing the perfect example of the qualities that make me special and unique."

Quintessential is an adjective from Latin 'quinta essentia' meaning 'fifth essence'; it describes someone or something that perfectly embodies the essential qualities of their class or type, referring to the ancient belief in a fifth element beyond earth, air, fire and water.

"I am RESILIENT, bouncing back from difficulties stronger than before, like a tree that bends but doesn't break in the wind."

Resilient is an adjective from Latin 'resilire' meaning 'to leap back'; it describes someone who recovers quickly from setbacks, suggesting both flexibility and inner strength that allows one to return to form after being compressed or stretched.

Sapient is an adjective from Latin 'sapiens' meaning 'wise'; it describes someone possessing wisdom and intelligence, connecting to the scientific name for humans (Homo sapiens) and emphasizing our capacity for deep understanding.

"I am SAPIENT, showing wisdom and good judgment in the choices I make and the way I understand the world."

Scrambled Words & Clues

1. **aSintpe** – A person who is very wise and full of knowledge.

2. **ieouariPpcscs** – Someone who understands things quickly and clearly.

3. **stAtue** – Someone who is clever and can figure things out fast.

4. **oausucidA** – Someone who is bold and not afraid to take risks. oceiZt – Full of life and energy.

5. **Rtlisneie** – Someone who stays strong, even when things get tough.

6. **zlanvniGgai** – Something that excites and inspires people to take action.

7. **vitpaitnagC** – So interesting that people can't stop watching or listening.

How to Play

- Unscramble each word to find the real word.

- Use the clues (word definitions) to help you.

- Once you solve them all, try using each word in your own sentence.

Bonus Challenge: Write a short story using at least three of the words from any set.

The Champion's Quest: An Affirmation Adventure! 🏆🌟

How to Play:

When challenges come your way, use positive, powerful words instead of negative ones! Fill in the blanks with encouraging words from the list below to remind yourself how awesome you are!

Words to Use (Encouraging Synonyms!):

1. Sapient (Instead of saying "I don't know enough," say "I am wise and capable!")

2. Felicitous (Instead of saying "I don't belong," say "I am exactly where I'm meant to be!")

3. Unfathomable (Instead of saying "I am not special," say "I have endless potential!")

4. Yare (Instead of saying "I'm too slow," say "I am quick and ready for action!")

5. Zoetic (Instead of saying "I feel unimportant," say "I am full of life and energy!")

6. Labyrinthine (Instead of saying "This problem is too hard," say "I can navigate any challenge!")

The Champion's Quest! ⚔️🏅

Deep in the heart of a magical land, a grand tournament was about to begin. Warriors from all over the world had gathered, but one stood out—the courageous champion, Oladapo.

As Oladapo prepared, he thought, "I am (1) _____, and my knowledge and wisdom will guide me through every challenge."

The first trial was a puzzle of twisting paths and tricky illusions. Most people would feel lost, but Oladapo smiled and thought, "I am (2) _____, and I am exactly where I need to be."

The next challenge was a test of endurance—crossing a river of shifting stones. Oladapo's strength and determination shone as he leaped from rock to rock. "I am (3) _____," Oladapo thought. "My power has no limits!"

Then, a sudden horn blast signaled the final challenge—a race against the fastest competitors in the land. Without hesitation, Oladapo burst forward, thinking, "I am (4) _____, quick and ready for anything!"

As he neared the finish line, the crowd erupted in cheers. Oladapo could feel their energy and excitement. "I am (5) _____," they thought. "I bring light and energy wherever I go!"

At last, standing victorious before the kingdom, Oladapo realized that this journey had been full of twists and turns, but he had faced it all with confidence. "I am (6) _____," he declared. "No challenge is too complicated for me!"

And so, the champion's name became legendary—forever known as the hero who believed in himself!

Your Challenge: Fill in the blanks with the words from the list and read your completed story out loud. Let these words remind you how smart, strong, and full of life you are!

✨ **Bonus Challenge:** Design your own tournament! What challenges would you include? How would you test a champion's courage?

Word Unscramble Challenge 3

Can you unscramble these words? Use the clues (word definitions) to help you solve them.

Scrambled Words & Clues

1. **ucAisouad** – Someone who is bold and not afraid to take risks.

2. **iQelnnssetatiu** – The perfect example of something.

3. **Ristienle** – Someone who stays strong, even when things are tough.

4. **ziinnlGaagv** – Something that excites and inspires people to take action.

5. **alioXdcohne** – A person who is friendly to strangers and guests.

6. **raeY** – Quick and ready to move or act.

7. **Laneirthibny** – Something very complex, like a confusing maze.

8. **inaapCgttiv** – So interesting that people can't stop watching or listening.

How to Play

- Unscramble each word to find the real word.
- Use the clues (word definitions) to help you.
- Once you solve them all, try using each word in your own sentence.

Bonus Challenge: Write a short story using at least three of the words from any set.

I am WONDROUS, filled with marvel and amazement that inspires others to see the magic in everyday things."

Wondrous is an adjective from the Old English 'wundor' meaning 'miracle'; it describes something that arouses awe or astonishment, suggesting the ability to both experience and create moments of wonder.

Xenodochial is an adjective derived from Greek 'xenos' (stranger) and 'doche' (reception); it describes someone who is warmly receptive to strangers or guests, emphasizing the special quality of being able to make others feel at home.

"I am **XENODOCHIAL**, friendly and kind to newcomers and strangers, making everyone feel welcome in my presence."

"I am YARE, quick and ready to respond to new opportunities with nimble energy and enthusiasm."

Yare is an archaic adjective from Old English 'gearu' meaning 'ready'; it describes someone who is quick, agile and responsive, originally used to describe ships that were easy to maneuver.

"I am ZOETIC, fully alive and living with vibrant energy that brings vitality to everything I do."

Zoetic is an adjective from Greek 'zōē' meaning 'life'; it describes something living or vital, emphasizing the quality of being animated with life force and vigor rather than merely existing.

Word search 3

```
I H E E N X I U S U O I C A C I P S R E P G U E T B O Q
I R E S I L I E N T D A K U J F C I X W S U P L H E F U
H U M A N I T A R I A N P K J E S A P I E N T B O R U N
L Q C T P P X G I D U G N I T A V I T P A C Y A Y O B F
P Q E T B W H X U E A Z L T J O K X W D L F D T Z L T A
A D L R A I T P L C V U S F H N F F P P A I I F U Y T
O S H K H M H N T E N A C I O U S E W T E I B M L D E H
X F G Q X H Q U A R Y M B W I M F L T O X S T O Y C U O
B V C Q M U S U U V W L L N T Q E I L D I O V D M P E M
T Y E H C I F Y Z D R E X E S D A C U E U Z E N S Z L A
P R U A N Z W K S I D E J G E U O I P B J Q W I V M I B
Z S S E N G O X X G L R S R U P F T U P O F S E U R E L
N D L K Y R E K E I J W E B N I I O H F O U R L A Y R E
K I Y V W G E A X R Y W D X O Z Y U J R O A T H I S A X
U S H E X A B P R F O A T A O Q Q S X R C I W G N S P A
Z C J C G L R D A P Q I N H A O Y E D I F Z S G U V N Y
J E K A E V G S M N I Z E A P H Z N O A Z U G O L V O C
U R P J Q A O E K A L Y L E I U O U C A S Z I M Y B N F
D N C I D N C E U X K A O R G W S E H V M C H I U D O P
I I M R F I N R X N M Z V A A S T U T E A J X Q F N G L
C N Z A A Z B E F O U V E Y K E R Q H D P J Y K W A U E
I G B K Y I J U I A X U N T D M D B U S B I U V R T N M
O A U T P N P C C W B A E H Q A I A K L Z N I E G C O E
U S L Z W G V Y N A M R B S G V J U Z O Q B Q Z T E P R
S U O X Q R F G Z O E T I C M D M E B T F O M A U N O U
G O L O O Z V A W C B O Z E R T Q S U T G Q M G T Z S S
K W L A B Y R I N T H I N E M J V F T F S H K Q G F E O
L A I T N E S S E T N I U Q L A I H C O D O N E X E M I
```

AUDACIOUS	HUMANITARIAN	OBSERVANT	UNFATHOMABLE
ASTUTE	INDOMITABLE	PERSPICACIOUS	VERACIOUS
BENEVOLENT	JUDICIOUS	QUINTESSENTIAL	WONDROUS
CAPTIVATING	KNOWLEDGEABLE	RESILIENT	XENODOCHIAL
EMPOWERED	LABYRINTHINE	SAPIENT	YARE
FELICITOUS	MULTIFACETED	TENACIOUS	ZOETIC
GALVANIZING	NONPAREIL		

How to Play:

13 **Find the Words:** Look for words hidden in the letter grid.

14 **Words Go Different Ways:** Words can go across, up and down, or diagonally. They can even be spelled backwards!

15 **Mark the Words:** When you find a word, circle it with a crayon or pencil.

16 **Tip:** Start by looking for the first letter of each word.

17 **You Win:** When you find all the words!

The words to look for are above

Complete the crossword puzzle below (J–R)

Down

1. A person who understands things very quickly and clearly.
2. The perfect example of something.
3. A person or thing that has many sides or talents, like an actor who can sing, dance, and act.
4. Something or someone that is the best at what they do, with no equal.
6. Someone who bounces back and stays strong even when things are tough.
7. Having or showing sound judgment; wise

Across

5. Someone who knows a lot about many things and loves to learn.
8. Someone who notices small details that others might miss.
9. This word describes something that is tricky to find your way through, like a giant maze.

Complete the Crossword puzzle below (S–Z)

Across

5. person who is friendly to strangers and guests.
7. A person who is wise and full of knowledge.
8. Full of life and energy.

Down

1. A person who always tells the truth.
2. Something amazing, exciting, and full of wonder.
3. Someone who never gives up, no matter how hard things get.
4. Something so big or strange that it's hard to understand.
6. Quick and ready to move or act.

Comic book
(write & draw your own story)

Answer keys
Word search 1

							N	O	N	P	A	R	E	I	L							
	E																				I	G
	S	N							D	E	R	E	W	O	P	M	E		N		N
		U	I						A	S	T	U	T	E		D				I
			O	H											O				T
			I	T									M					A
		D			C	N							I					V
		E			I	I					T						I
A		T				D	R	N	A	I	R	A	T	I	N	A	M	U	H	T
U		E			E			U	Y			B								P
D		C	G		L				J	B	L									A
A		A	A		B					E	A									C
C		F	L		A	E				F	E	L	I	C	I	T	O	U	S	
I		I	V		E		N										
O		T	A		G			E									
U		L	N		D				V								
S		U	I		E					O							
		M	Z		L					L							
			I		W						E						
			N		O						N					
			G		N							T					
					K												

Word search 2

Word search 3

```
. . . . . . . . S U O I C A C I P S R E P . . E . . . .
. R E S I L I E N T . . . . . . . . . . . . . L . . . U
H U M A N I T A R I A N . . . . S A P I E N T B . . . N
. . . . . . . . . . . . G N I T A V I T P A C . A . . F
. . . . . . . . . . . . . . K . . . . . . . . T . . . A
. . . . . . T . . . . . . . N . F . . . . . . I . . . T
. . . . . . . N T E N A C I O U S E . . . . . M . . . H
. . . . . . . . A . . . . W . . L . . . . . O . . . . O
. . . . . . . . . V . L . . . . I . . . . . D . . . . M
. . . . . . . . . . R E . . . D . C . . . . N . . L . A
. . . . . . . . . . D E . . E . . . I . . . . I V M I B
. . . . . . . . . G . . S R . . . T . . . . S E U . E L
. D . . . . . . E . . . E B . . . . O . . . U R L . . R E
. I . . . . G . A . . . W . . O . . . U . . O A T . . . A .
. S . . . A B . . . O . T . . . . S . R C I . . . S P .
. C . . L . . . P . N . . . . D I F . . . U . N .
J E . . E V . . M . . . E . . . . N O A . . . O . . O .
U R . . . A . E . . . . L E . . O U C . . . I . . . N .
D N . . . N . . . . . . O R . W S E . . . . C . . . . .
I I . . . . I . . . . . V A A S T U T E A . . . . . . .
C N . . . Z . . . . . . E Y . E . . . . D . . . . . . .
I G . . . I . . . . . . N . D . . . . U . . . . . . . .
O . . . . N . . . . . . E . . . . A . . . . . . . . . .
U . . . . G . . . . . . B . . . . . . . . . . . . . . .
S . . . . . . Z O E T I C . . . . . . . . . . . . . . .
. . . . . . . . . . . . . . . . . . . . . . . . . . . .
. . L A B Y R I N T H I N E . . . . . . . . . . . . . .
L A I T N E S S E T N I U Q L A I H C O D O N E X . . .
```

About Pocketlings

Hi! I'm Olamide!

I created Pocketlings because I thought it would be super cool if kids could learn about different people. I'm from Nigeria, Canada, and America, so I know what it's like when people are different but still awesome!

I make stuff for kids that shows them all the amazing different kinds of people in the world. It's like when you mix different colors and get something way prettier! I hope my books and toys help kids see that being different is actually really great!

You can see more and stay updated at https://www.pocketlings.com

www.ingramcontent.com/pod-product-compliance
Lightning Source LLC
Chambersburg PA
CBHW042301030526
44119CB00066B/842